ISLAM

What is **Islam**?
Is Islam a new **Religion**?
What is the distinctive **Feature** of Islam?
How does Islam relate to **Mankind**?

MUSLIMS

Who are the **Muslims**?
What are the **Pillars of Faith**?
Why Muslims use the word **'Allah'** instead of **'God'**?
How does someone become a **Muslim**?

PROPHETHOOD

What is **Prophethood** in Islam?
Who is **Muhammad**?
What is **Sunnah**?
What does Islam say about **Torah** and **Bible**?
How Islam views **Judaism and Christianity**?
What does Islam say about **Original Sin**?
What does Islam say about **Jesus**?

QUR'AN

What is the **Qur'an**?
Does Islam recognize **Science and Technology**?

WORSHIP

What is **Worship** in Islam?
What are the **Five Pillars** of Islam?
What is the **Ka'bah**?

COMMUNITY

What are **Human Rights** in Islam?
What is **Jihad** in Islam?
What is **Hijaab** (Islamic Dress Code)?
How does Islam view **Family Life**?
What is the **Status of Women** in Islam?
What is **Marriage** in Islam?
Why is **More than One Wife** permitted in Islam?
What does Islam say about **Parents and the Elderly**?
What does Islam say about **Food**?
What does Islam say about **Intoxicants and Gambling**?
What Islam say about **Business Interaction**?

CONCEPTS

What is the concept of **God** in Islam?
What is the concept of **Life** in Islam?
What is the concept of **Life after Death** in Islam?
What is the concept of **Sin** in Islam?

1

*In the name of Allah (God), the
Compassionate, the Merciful*

What is Islam?

Islam is an Arabic word which means
peace, submission and obedience. It
also means acceptance and commitment to abide by the teachings and
guidance of God. One of the beautiful
names of God is As-Salâm (The Peace).
Islam also means to be at peace with
God and His creatures. Being at peace
with God implies complete submission
to His will, Who is the source of all
purity and goodness. Being at peace
with His creatures implies living in
peace within one's self, with other
people and with the environment.
Thus, Islam is a total system of living
in peace. Islam is the same message
and guidance which God revealed
through all His Prophets to every
people throughout the history of
mankind. One who follows Islam
is called a Muslim (an Arabic word
which means, the one who submits to
the will of God).

Is Islam a new
Religion?

No! It is the same religion which was
preached by all the prophets and
is further elaborated through the
Prophet Muhammad, peace be upon
him. God ordered him:

*"Say: We believe in Allah and in that
which was revealed to us, and in that which
was revealed to Abraham and Ishmael and
Isaac and Jacob and the tribes and in that*

*which was given to Moses and to Jesus
and to other Prophets from their God; we
make no distinction between any of them,
and to Him we are Muslims."*
Al-Qur'an 3:84

The religion of Islam is as old as
humanity itself. It was in fact the
religion of every prophet of God,
who appeared in any part of the
world. According to the Qur'an,
Islam was the religion of Adam, Noah,
Abraham, Ishmael, Isaac, Jacob, Moses
and Jesus, peace be upon them all.
However, it was revealed to Prophet
Muhammad, peace be upon him, in
its comprehensive, complete and final
form.

What is the
distinctive Feature of
Islam?

The major characteristic of Islam is that
through believing in all the Prophets
and God's message revealed to each of
them; it lays down the basis of peace
and harmony among the people of the
world.

The great mission of Islam is not only
to preach the above-mentioned truth,
but also to correct those errors which
had crept into the prevailing religions.
Most important of all, Islam gathers in
one book all those truths which were
contained in earlier Divine revelations
granted to previous Prophets for the
guidance of mankind, and to meet all
the spiritual and moral requirements
of an ever-advancing humanity.

Muslims are encouraged to cooperate
with all those who are faithful and
God-conscious people, namely those
who received scriptures (Torah,
Psalms and Gospel) through His

Prophets. Christians and Jews are called the "People of the Book," and their Prophets and Scriptures are honored by the Muslims.

How Islam relates to Mankind?

Islam teaches that diversity among human beings is a sign of God's mercy and no one has superiority based on one's color, language or nationality.

Islam promotes the brotherhood of man, toleration of one another, sympathy for the unfortunate and cooperation for general human happiness. If there is any one religion in the world which has strove to eliminate racism, it is Islam. There is no distinction between men on account of mere birth in a partic ular family, particular profession, particular race or particular country, and that all human beings are equal. God created people of different colors, nationalities, languages and ethnic origins so that we may recognize one another.

In Islam, superiority is based on the love and fear of God, doing good deeds, and maintaining high moral and spiritual qualities. In many respects Islam has regulated the relationships between men regardless of creeds, races or colors. One of the aims of Islam is to emphasize the oneness of humanity as a whole

and also the Oneness of the Creator of mankind and of all beings. Islam pronounces loudly, clearly, and with great emphasis that all people are, by nature, equal in all respects and that no one is better or superior to anyone else except through piety.

Who are the Muslims?

Muslims are those 1.9 billion people (per CIA World's Facts Book in year 2000), from all races, colors, nationalities and cultures who believe in One God (Allah) and accept Muhammad, peace be upon him, as the last Prophet. The majority of Muslims live in Indonesia, Bangladesh, Pakistan, Afghanistan, Iran, Turkey, Iraq, Syria, Jordan, Palestine, Egypt, Libya, Algeria, Morocco, Bosnia and other parts of the continents of Asia and Africa. Significant minorities are in India, China, Russia, Europe, North America (over 9.993 million in the USA) and South America.

A Muslim is a person who freely and willingly accepts the supreme power of God and strives to organize his or her life in accordance with His commandments. Hence a Muslim is any person anywhere in the world whose obedience, allegiance, and loyalty are to the One and Only God (Allah), the Creator of the Universe, and as such submits to the Divine Laws following the Sunnah (traditions) of the Prophet Muhammad, peace be upon him.

My Lord! Let me die as a Muslim and count me among the righteous

COUNTRY
Muslim Population by

- < 3%
- 3%-6%
- 7%-20%
- 21%-100%

What are the Pillars of Imaan (Faith)?

Muslims believe in:

- One and Only God (Allah) with all His unique attributes;

- Angels created by Him;

- All the Holy Books originally revealed to the different Prophets, including the Torah, Psalms, Gospel (Bible) and the Qur'an;

- All the Prophets through whom God sent His Message to mankind including Noah, Abraham, Ishmael, Isaac, Jacob, Joseph, Moses, David, Jesus and Muhammad, peace be upon them all;

- The Day of Judgment (the Day of Resurrection - Life after Death) and individual's accountability (reward and punishment) for good and bad deeds / actions; and

- Al-Qadar (God's Pre-estimation), which means God knows everything. He knows what has happened and what will happen.

Why Muslims use the word 'Allah' instead of 'God'?

The word 'Allah' is the combination of two Arabic words 'AL Ilâh' which means 'The God'; it is the proper name of the only Supreme Being Who exists necessarily by Himself. This word comprises all the attributes of perfection. This word is neither feminine nor plural and has never been applied to any other being. This word has no corresponding word in English or in any other language of the world. Allah is the One and Only True God's personal name. Nothing or no one else can be called Allah. That is why Muslims use the word Allah, His personal name, and not God.

It is interesting to note that Allah is also used for God in Aramaic, the language of Jesus, peace be upon him, and that all Arab Jews and Christians also use the word Allah for God.

How can someone become a Muslim?

Anyone who believes in One God and does not consider any other deity worthy of worship besides Him, all he or she has to do is to affirm the belief in the last Prophet of God Muhammad, peace be upon him through saying:

La Ilaha Illallahu Muhammad-ur-Rasoollallah

'There is no deity (god) except Allah (the One and Only True God) and Muhammad is the Messenger of Allah,' and then follow the Qur'an and traditions of the Prophet Muhammad, peace be upon him. This is called the Shahadah (bearing witness to the Truth).

What is Prophethood in Islam?

The Merciful and Loving God not only created human beings, but also arranged for their guidance through appointing Prophets throughout the ages from among the human beings. God revealed His will to the Prophets, peace be upon them all, and commissioned them to deliver that Message. In every known nation one or more Prophets were appointed. All the prophets of God were men of good character and high honor. Their honesty and truthfulness, their intelligence and integrity were beyond doubt.

The appointment of these Prophets from God is a clear manifestation of a strong link between Heaven and Earth, between God and man. The purpose of Prophethood is to confirm what mankind already knows or can know, and to teach them what they do not or cannot know by their own means. Such as: why we are created? What will happen to us after death? Is there any life after death? Are we accountable for our actions? Similarly questions about God, Angels, paradise, and hell cannot be answered without revelations from the Creator and Knower of the unseen. It is also to help man to find the Right Path, and to do what is right and shun what is wrong. Prophethood is an eloquent expression of God's love for human beings and His will to guide them to the right way of belief and behavior. He provides true guidance to mankind, and then holds them responsible for their deeds. He gave them warnings through His prophets about the consequences of their wrongful deeds, and the good news of rewards for their good deeds.

The Source of Prophethood and the appointment of all the prophets is One and the Same: it is the One and Only God (Allah). The Prophet's aim is to serve God, to acquaint human beings with God and His Divine teachings, to establish truth and goodness, to help mankind realize the true purpose of their existence and to help them in living their lives in a purposeful way. It is on this basis that the Muslims make no distinction among any of the Prophets and accept their teachings as consistent and complementary to each other.

Who is Muhammad?

Muhammad, peace be upon him, is the last Prophet of God appointed for the guidance of the whole of mankind. He is answer to the prayer of Prophets

Abraham and Ishmael, peace be upon them:

"Our Lord, appoint from among them (residents of Makkah) a Messenger who shall recite to them Your Revelations and teach them the Book and the Wisdom, and purify them; surely, You are the All-Mighty, the Wise." Al-Qur'an 2:129

His appointment is foretold by the Prophet Jesus, peace be upon him:

"And remember when Isa (Jesus) the son of Mary said: "O children of Israel! I am the Messenger of Allah towards you, confirming the Torah which came before me, and giving you good news of a Messenger that will come after me whose name shall be Ahmad (another name of the Prophet Muhammad)." Al-Qur'an 61:6

He was born in 570 AD in Makkah, Arabia. As he grew up he became known for his honesty and truthfulness and people used to call him Al-Ameen (the trustworthy) and Al-Sâdiq (the truthful). He was very calm and meditative. He had no ambition for becoming a leader. He used to go away from the city crowd and meditate in a cave called Hira on a nearby barren mountain.

Cave of Hira at the Mountain of Light

It was in this secluded place where God sent him the first revelation through Angel Gabriel when he was forty years old. It is important to note that he could neither read nor write.

Muhammad, peace be upon him, is a human being who was chosen by God and assigned the mission of leading humanity to righteousness, and serving as a model of moral conduct. In this role, Muhammad peace be upon him, did experience the difficulties and trials which all Prophets before him experienced.

O Prophet! Surely, We have sent you as a witness, as a bearer of good news and as a Warner, and to call the people towards Allah

As soon as he began to recite the revelations he received from God, he and his small group of followers suffered bitter persecution. Finally in the year 622 A.D. (after 13 years of preaching), God gave him permission to immigrate from Makkah to a city over 200 miles away called Yathrib which is now known as Al-Madinah. This migration, called the Hijra, marks the beginning of the Islamic calendar.

Masjid Nabwi – Madinah, Saudi Arabia

Of all the Prophets of Allah, Prophet Muhammad, peace be upon him, is the only one whose life is well documented in the historical records. Although Jesus, peace be upon him, lived only

2,000 years ago in an important part of the Roman Empire, the Empire was at its prime and had many eminent historians and writers recording every development, but no early historian mentioned the birth, the mission and the crucifixion of Jesus, peace be upon him. Only one Jewish historian, Josephus, made a casual reference, which is considered to be a later addition.

Inside view of Masjid Nabwi - Madinah

It is part of human nature to look to someone higher and nobler for guidance to make him one's role model. Muhammad, peace be upon him, is an exemplar. The life of Muhammad is like an open book from cover to cover; from his posthumous birth to his childhood, to his youth, to his Prophethood, to his being the ruler of Arabia and finally right up to his death. One non-Muslim scholar, Lamartine, writes the following words about him:

"If greatness of purpose, smallness of means, and astounding results are the three criteria of human genius, who could dare to compare any great man in modern history with Muhammad. The most famous men created arms, laws and empires only. They founded, if anything at all, no more than material powers which often crumbled away before their eyes. This man moved not only armies, legislations, empires, people and dynasties but millions of men in one-third of the then inhabited world; and more than that, he moved the altars, the gods, the religions, the ideas, the beliefs and souls. On the basis of a Book, every letter of which has become law, he created a spiritual nationality, which blended together people of every tongue and of every race. He has left for us as the indelible characteristic of this Muslim nationality, the hatred of false gods and the passion for the one and immaterial God. Philosopher, Orator, apostle, legislator, warrior, conqueror of ideas, restorer of rational dogmas, of a cult without images, the founder of twenty terrestrial empires and of one spiritual empire, that is Muhammad. As regards all standards by which human greatness may be measured we may well ask, is there any man greater than he is?"

Historledela Turquie, Paris.
Vol.II, pp.276-277

What is Sunnah?

Sunnah is the sayings, actions and tacit approval of the Prophet Muhammad, peace be upon him. It is another source of Islamic Laws, rules and regulations, and ranks second after the Qur'an. Sunnah is recorded in books of Hadith (narrations) and is important in understanding the meaning of the Qur'anic text, exploring the principles outlined in the Qur'an and showing how to understand and practice them.

Examples of Prophet's sayings:

No one can be a believer until he wishes for his brother what he wishes for himself.

It is not befitting for a believer to sever his relationship (not be on speaking terms) with his brother for more than three days.

The one who is ungrateful to others is ungrateful to God.

When the leader of a Community comes to you, receive him with due respect.

Actions (and deeds) are judged (by God) based on one's intentions.

The best approach in everything is moderation.

This world is a prison for the believer and paradise for the unbeliever.

In forgiveness of a king lies the survival of his kingdom.

Muhammad is the Messenger of Allah

The upper hand (giving) is better than the lower hand (receiving).

True Muslim is the one from whose tongue and hands other Muslims are safe.

What does Islam say about Torah and Bible (Injeel / Gospel)?

Islam requires the Muslims to believe in all the prior scriptures including Taurat (Torah) and Injeel (Gospel/ Bible) that they were the true revelations from Allah. Because of not preserving in original languages in written form and translating them in various languages from oral narrations through centuries, human words were mingled with Divine Words, therefore, they lost their pure forms. Relating to this fact the Holy Qur'an states:

Then in the footsteps of those Prophets (Abraham, Isaac, Jacob, David, Moses and

others), We sent Jesus, the son of Mary, confirming whatever remained intact from the Torah in his time, and gave him the Injeel (Gospel/Bible) wherein was guidance and light, confirming what was revealed in the Torah; a guidance and an admonition to those who fear Allah. Therefore, let the people who follow the Injeel (Gospel/Bible), judge by the Law which Allah has revealed therein; those who do not judge by the Law which Allah has revealed, are indeed the transgressors. To you (O Muhammad), We have revealed this Book (Al-Qur'an) with the truth. It confirms whatever has remained intact from the Book which came before it (Gospel/ Bible) and also to safeguard it. Therefore, judge between them according to Allah's revelations and do not yield to their vain desires, diverging from the truth which has come to you. We have ordained a law and a Way of life for each of you. If Allah wanted, He could have made all of you a single nation. But He willed otherwise in order to test you in what He has given you; therefore, try to excel one another in good deeds. (Ultimately) you all shall return to Allah; then He will tell you the truth of those matters in which you dispute.
                    Al-Qur'an 5:46-48

How Islam views Judaism and Christianity?

Islam calls Jews and Christians as 'the People of the Book' to whom came the great Prophets including Moses (Musa) and Jesus (Isa). Islam invites them to cooperate in what is common between them and Islam. In the respective Prophets' time they were also called Muslims as God Almighty said in the Holy Qur'an about Prophet Abraham, the forefather of Moses and Jesus, peace be upon them, in the following words:

Say: "O people of the Book! Let us get together on what is common between us and you: that we shall worship none but Allah (the One and only True God); that we shall not associate any partners with Him; that we shall not take from among ourselves any lords beside Allah." If they reject your invitation then tell them: "Bear witness that we are Muslims (who have surrendered to Allah)." O people of the Book! Why do you argue with us about Abraham as to whether he was a Jew or a Christian? You know that the Torah and the Gospel were revealed long after him? Have you no sense at all? So far, you have been arguing about things of which you had some knowledge! Must you now argue about that of which you know nothing at all? Allah knows while you do not. Abraham was neither a Jew nor a Christian but he was a Muslim, true in faith. He was not one of the Mushrikeen (who set up partners with Allah).

Al-Qur'an 3: 64-67

have believed, they shall be rightly guided; if they reject it, they will surely fall into dissension (divide into differing factions); Allah will be your sufficient defender against them, and He hears and knows everything.

Baptism is the baptism of Allah; and who is better than Allah in baptizing? Him do we worship.

Door of Ka'bah

Say (O Muhammad): "Would you dispute with us concerning Allah, who is our Lord and your Lord as well? We shall be accountable to Him for our deeds and you for yours; to Him Alone we are devoted. Do you claim that Abraham, Ishmael, Isaac, Jacob and their descendants were all Jews or Christians? Say: Are you more knowledgeable than Allah?" Who is more unjust than the one who hides the testimony received from Allah? Allah is not unaware of what you do.

Al-Qur'an 2:136-140

Muslims are required to believe in all the Holy Scriptures revealed to various Prophets in the following words:

Say: "We believe in Allah and that which is revealed to us; and what was revealed to Abraham, Ishmael, Isaac, Jacob and their descendants, and that which was given to Moses, Jesus and other Prophets from their Lord. We make no distinction between any of them, and to Him (Allah) we have surrendered ourselves (in Islam)." So, if they believe (accept Islam) like you

Muslims are allowed to eat the food and marry chaste women from the People of the Book. What can be more intimate relationship than husband and wife - basic unit of future generations. God says in the Holy Qur'an:

Today all good clean things have been made lawful for you; and the food of the People of the Book (Jews and Christians) is also made lawful for you and your food is made lawful for them. Likewise, marriage with chaste free believing women and also chaste women among the People who were *given the Book before you is made lawful for you, provided that you give them their dowries and desire chastity, neither committing fornication nor taking them as mistresses. Anyone who commits Kufr with Imân (rejects faith), all his good deeds will become void (zero) and in the hereafter, he will be among the losers.*

Al-Qur'an 5: 5

What does Islam say about Original Sin?

Islam says that every soul is born sin free. When a child grows up and is able to distinguish between right and wrong, sin and virtue and intentionally does something wrong or commits a sinful act then he/she commits the first sin. Regarding this the Holy Qur'an states:

By the soul and He (God) Who perfected it and inspired it with knowledge of what is wrong for it and what is right for it: indeed successful will be the one who purifies it, and indeed unsuccessful will be the one who corrupts it!   Al-Qur'an 91:7-10

Everyone will bear the burden of one's own sin and no one will be held for the sin of another:

Say: "Should I seek another Lord besides Allah when He is the Lord of everything?" Every soul will reap the fruits of its own deeds; no bearer of burdens shall bear the burden of another. Ultimately you will return to your Lord, and He will resolve for you your disputes.

Al-Qur'an 6:164

He that seeks guidance, that guidance shall be for his own soul, but he that goes astray does so to his own loss. No bearer shall bear the burden of another (on the Day of Judgment), We do not inflict punishment until We send forth a Messenger (to make

truth distinct from falsehood).

Al-Qur'an 17:15

Following is the prayer of Adam and Eve, peace be upon them, which they made, after they were sent down on earth, seeking forgiveness for their sin of disobedience to God:

Our Lord! We have wronged our souls. If You do not forgive us and have mercy on us, we shall certainly be among the losers.

When they repented, God forgave their sin of disobedience. The Holy Qur'an states:

But Satan (tempted them to disobey Allah's commandment) and caused them to slip therefrom (paradise), and get them expelled from where they were. We said: "Get down from here, some of you being enemies to others, and there is for you in the earth an abode and provisions for a specified period." Then Adam received appropriate words from his Lord and repented, and (Allah) accepted his repentance. Surely, He is the Acceptor of Repentance, the Merciful.

Al-Qur'an 2:36-37

Islam says that all children that die before the age they could distinguish between right and wrong shall enter Paradise. This is where Islam differs with Christianity:

The church holds that all unbaptised people, including new born babies who died, would go to hell. This was because original sin - the punishment that God inflicted on humanity because of Adam and

Eve's disobedience - had not been cleansed by baptism. Father Brian Harrison, a theologian, argues that the clear "doctrine of the Catholic Church for two millennia has been that wherever the souls of such infants do go, they definitely don't go to heaven."

BBC's Religion and Ethics Website

He said, O my Lord! Grant me a righteous child as Your special favor; surely, You hear all prayers.

What does Islam say about Jesus?

In Islam Jesus, peace be upon him, was a Prophet of God the same as Noah, Abraham, David, Moses and Muhammad, peace be upon them all. He was a human being, son of Mary and born miraculously without a father. His example is like that of Adam born without a mother or father and so was Jesus, peace be upon him, born without a father. These examples are from the signs of God to show mankind that He, the Almighty, does not need parents to create if He so Wills. Muslims believe in Jesus, peace be upon him, as a Prophet of God; they respect and revere him to the extent that they never mention him simply as Jesus but add the words 'peace be upon him.' There is a full chapter in the Holy Qur'an called "Mary" (Chapter 19).

Mary, may Allah be pleased with her, is considered among the purest women in the whole world. As for Jesus, peace be upon him, God says in the Qur'an:

These are the Messengers (which We have sent for the guidance of mankind). We have exalted some above others. To some Allah spoke directly; others He raised in ranks; to Isa (Jesus) the son of Mary, We gave Clear Signs and supported him with the Holy Spirit. Al-Qur'an 2:253

The Qur'an describes the birth of Jesus, peace be upon him, and the miracles given to him as follows:

Behold! When the angels said "O Mary! God gives you the good news with a Word from Him that you will be given a son: his name will be Messiah, Isa (Jesus) the son of Mary. He will be noble in this world and the Hereafter; and he will be from those who are very close to God. He will speak to the people in the cradle and in his old age and he will be among the righteous." Hearing this, Mary said, "O my Lord! How can I have a son when no man has ever touched me?" He replied, "Even so, Allah creates however He wants; whenever He decides to do anything, He only says to it, 'Be,' and it is! God will teach your son the Book, the Wisdom, the Torah, and the Injeel (Gospel) and send him forth as a Prophet to the Children of Israel with this message: 'I have brought you signs of my appointment from your Lord. I will make for you the likeness of a bird from clay; I will breathe into it and, with God's leave, it will become a living bird. I will heal the blind and the lepers, and raise the dead to life, by God's leave. Furthermore, I will tell you what you have eaten and what you have stored in your houses. Surely these are the signs to convince you if you are believers. Al-Qur'an 3:45-49

About the status of Jesus, peace be

upon him, God says:

O People of the Book! Do not transgress the limits of your religion. Speak nothing but the Truth about God. The Messiah, Jesus the son of Mary was no more than a Prophet of God and His Word (Be) which He bestowed on Mary and a Spirit from Him (which took the shape of a child in her womb). So, believe in God and His Prophet and do not say: "Trinity"." Stop saying that, it is better for you. God is only One Deity. He is far above from the need of having a son! To Him belong all that is in the Heavens and in the Earth. God alone is sufficient for their protection.

Al-Qur'an 4:171

While pointing out the innovations and changes made by the Jews and Christians in their religions and their claim about the divinity and crucifixion of Jesus, peace be upon him, the Holy Qur'an has stated the following facts:

They (Jews) went in their unbelief to such an extent that they uttered terrible slander against Mary. They even say: "We have killed the Messiah, Isa (Jesus), son of Mary, the Prophet of God." Whereas in fact, neither did they kill him nor did they crucify him but they thought they did (because the matter was made dubious for them). Those who differ therein are only in doubt. They know nothing about it but follow mere conjectures, for they were not sure that they did actually succeeded in killing Jesus. Nay! The fact is that God raised him up to Himself. God is Mighty, Wise. There are none of the People of the Book but will believe in this before his death; and on the Day of Resurrection Jesus will bear witness against them.

Al-Qur'an 4: 156-159

On the Day of Judgment God will ask Jesus, peace be upon him, to testify about his own statements and the misunderstandings attributed to him

by the Christians; this dialogue is documented in the Holy Qur'an in the following words:

(On the Day of Judgment) God will ask: "O Isa (Jesus) son of Mary, Did you ever say to the people, "worship me and my mother as gods beside Allah (God)?" He will answer: "Glory to You! How could I say what I had no right to say? If I had ever said so, you would have certainly known it. You know what is in my heart, but I know not what is in Yours; for You have full knowledge of all the unseen. I never said anything other than what You commanded me to say, that is to worship Allah (God), Who is my Lord and your Lord. I was a witness over them as long as I remained among them; but when You recalled me, You were the Watcher over them and You are a Witness to everything. If You punish them they surely are Your servants; and if You forgive them, You are Mighty, Wise." Al-Qur'an 5: 116-118

Our Lord, do not let our hearts deviate from the truth after you have guided us, and grant us Your own mercy; You are the Grantor of bounties without measure.

What is the Qur'an?

The *Qur'an* is the last word of God revealed to the Prophet Muhammad, peace be upon him, through Angel Gabriel. It is the primary source of Islamic teachings and laws. It deals with the whole of human life including the basic beliefs of Islam, morality, worship, knowledge, wisdom, God-and-man relationship and relations with one another. Comprehensive teachings on which sound systems of social justice, politics, economics, legislation, jurisprudence, law and international relations can be built form an important part of the Holy Qur'an. The Qur'an was revealed to the Prophet Muhammad, peace be upon him, from God gradually on various occasions over a 23 year period to answer certain questions, solve certain problems, settle certain disputes, and to be man's best guide to the truth of God and eternal happiness. Every letter in the Qur'an is the word of God. Revealed in Arabic, it is still and will remain in its original and complete Arabic version, because God has made it His concern to preserve the Qur'an, to make it always the best guide for man, and to safeguard it against corruption. The Qur'an has 114 chapters called Sürahs, with over 6,000 verses.

In testimony to God's conservation, the Qur'an is the only Scripture in human history that has been preserved in its complete and original version without the slightest change in style or even punctuation. The history of recording the Qur'an, compiling its chapters and conserving its text is beyond any doubt. Of all religious books, the Qur'an alone has remained unaltered, unedited and unchanged. Whether or not non-Muslim scholars accept the Qur'an as the word of God, they are unanimous in the view that its language and its wording have remained in their original form. This is unique to Islam. All other divine books have been edited, rehashed and revised by their votaries with the passage of time. As a matter of fact, it is such a standing miracle bestowed

on Muhammad, peace be upon him, that if the whole of mankind were to work together they could not produce the like of one Qur'anic chapter.

The Holy Qur'an is neither only a book of law (though it contains the principles of the laws necessary for the guidance of mankind), nor merely a book of sacred history (though it contains the necessary sacred history). It is pre-eminently a book that manifests the glory, greatness, grandeur, goodness, love, purity, power and knowledge of God, the Supreme Being. This is the only book that is memorized by hundreds of thousands of Muslims. It is a living miracle that the whole book can be memorized word for word with punctuation.

The original and complete text of the Qur'an in Arabic and translations of its meaning in most known languages are available in major libraries, Islamic centers and bookstores.

Within a short period of twenty-three years its injunctions swept away the deep-rooted evils, like idolatry, drinking, gambling, adultery, fornication, child abuse, etc., from Arabia and anywhere Islam spread. It erased all traces of vices in the Arabian society and transformed ignorant people into the foremost torchbearers of knowledge and science. Every word of this Book gives expression to the

Divine Majesty and Glory, and Power in a manner which is not approached by any other religious book. The Holy Qur'an has challenged everyone, who has a doubt in its revelation from God, to produce one chapter like any chapter of this Holy Book. No one has been able do it.

Does Islam recognize Science and Technology?

Islam recognizes and encourages the use of science and the scientific methods. According to the Prophet Muhammad, peace be upon him, acquisition of knowledge is obligatory on every Muslim man and woman. In Islam, science and technology should be used for moral ends and serve all legitimate needs of mankind. Moreover, both are viewed as yet another means to understand and see the power and glory of God.

Read! Your Lord is the Most Gracious, Who taught by the Pen, taught man what he knew not. *Al-Qur'an 96:3-5*

Soon shall We show them Our signs in the universe and in their own souls, until it becomes clear to them that this Qur'an

is indeed the Truth. Is it not enough that your Lord is a witness over everything? *Al-Qur'an 41:53*

Based on the sayings of the Prophet Muhammad, peace be upon him, and the teachings of the Qur'an, Muslims of the early period of the Islamic era became pioneers in medicine, chemistry, physics, arts, astronomy, geography, navigation, poetry, mathematics, logarithms, calculus, architecture, literature, and history.

Islamic Architect: Taj Mahal – Agra in India

Arabic numerals, the concept of zero (which is vital to the advancement of mathematics) and algebra were developed and transmitted from Islamic states to Europe, which contributed to the Renaissance of Europe and world civilization. Muslims also developed sophisticated instruments like the astrolabe, the quadrant and good navigational maps.

What is Worship in Islam?

In Islam each and every action which is done in accordance with God's commandment is worship. Therefore, doing a job, raising a family, interaction with community are all acts of worship if done in accordance with God's commandments as acted upon and directed by the Prophet Muhammad, peace be upon him. Islam requires the individual to submit himself completely to Allah:

"Say, surely my prayer, my sacrifice, my life and my death are all for Allah, the Lord of the worlds, He has no partners; thus I am commanded, and I am the first of the Muslims." A-Qur'an 6:162-163

Inside of King Faisal Masjid Islamabad in Pakistan

Masjid Quba First Mosque of the Prophet in Madinah, Saudi Arabia

The natural result of this submission is that one's actions should conform to the instructions of the One to Whom the person is submitting. Islam requires that its followers model their lives according to its teachings in every respect.

Islam does not teach ritualism. It places great emphasis on intention and action. To worship God is to love Him and to act upon His commands in every aspect of life, to enjoin goodness and

forbid wrongdoing and oppression, to practice charity and justice and to serve Him by serving mankind. The Qur'an presents this sublime concept in the following words:

"It is not righteousness that you turn your faces to the East or the West, but righteous is he who believes in Allah and the Last Day and the Angels and the Book and the Prophets; and gives his wealth for love of Him to kinsfolk and to orphans and the needy and the wayfarer and to those who ask, and sets slaves free; and observes proper worship and pays the Zakah. And those who keep their treaty when they make one, and they are patient in tribulation, adversity and time of stress; such are those who are sincere. Such are the God-fearing." Al-Qur'an 2:177

What are the Five Pillars of Islam?

Every action done with the awareness that it fulfills the Will of God is considered an act of worship in Islam. But five specific acts of worship termed as the Pillars of Islam provide the framework of Muslim's spiritual life. These are: declaration of Faith, Prayers, Alms giving, Fasting and Pilgrimage to Makkah for those who can afford to do so physically and financially.

1. The Declaration of Faith:
To say:

La Ilaha Illallahu Muhammad-ur-Rasoollallah

"There is none worthy of worship except One God (Allah), and that Muhammad is His messenger."

It is called *Shahadah* (to bear witness). This is to affirm that God is One and that Muhammad, peace be upon him, is one of His Prophets. In other words, to make a commitment that one shall follow God's commandments and the exemplary life of the Prophet Muhammad, peace be upon him, in each and every respect.

2. Prayers *(Salat)* are prescribed five times a day as a duty towards God. Salat is the direct link between the worshipper and God. Salat and Zakat (2nd and 3rd pillar of Islam) have been mandatory in the Shari'ah (laws) of all prior prophets. The Holy Qur'an states the address of Jesus, peace be upon him, to his people at his birth:

Whereupon the baby (Jesus) spoke out: "I am indeed a servant of Allah. He has given me the Book (Gospel) and made me a Prophet. He has made me blessed wherever I may be. He has commanded me to establish Salah (prayer) and give Zakah (obligatory charity) as long as I live.
Al-Qur'an 19: 30-31

Salat (Prayer) is commanded for spiritual elevation of the individuals. It purifies the heart and controls temptation, wrongdoing, and evil. There is no priesthood in Islam, so the collective prayers are led by a learned person who knows the Qur'an, and is chosen by the congregation.

Prayers are offered the way the Prophet offered his prayers. Prayers are said in Arabic which include: praise to God, a few verses from the Holy Qur'an, salutation to the Prophet and supplication for oneself, one's parents, children, and the rest of the world.

Kuala Kangsar Mosque - Malaysia

Prayers are offered at dawn, afternoon, before sunset, after sunset and nightfall. Although it is preferable to offer the prayers in congregation in a mosque, a Muslim can pray at home or anywhere, such as in offices, factories and parks when it is the time to offer the prayer.

3. Almsgiving *(Zakat)* means 'purification' and it also means growth. Wealth is purified through setting aside a specified portion of one's wealth for the poor, needy, those who suffer losses from incidents beyond their control and the general welfare to establish economic balance and social justice in the society. Muslims are encouraged to spend in charity as much as they can beyond the mandatory requirement of Zakat which is called Sadaqah (voluntary charity).

It is important to note that Zakat is on savings held for one full year and is not on the money in circulation. In other words Islam encourages the Muslims to put their money in circulation so that everyone in the community can benefit from it. Those who hold capital from circulation are hurting the poor and the community's welfare projects. Therefore, The Prophet Muhammad (peace be upon him) ordered such persons to pay a minimum of one fortieth (two and a half percent) for the poor, needy and community welfare projects.

Zakat is an act of worship for the wealth of a believer and plays an important role in providing financial stability to the community. The Prophet Muhammad, peace be upon him, said: "Zakah is the treasure of Islam." One of the main reasons for poverty in the Muslim countries is neglecting this pillar of Islam.

4. Fasting (Sawm) during the month of Ramadan: This means abstention from food, beverages, and sex from dawn to sunset, and curbing evil intentions, desires and actions. Those who are sick, on a journey, too old, and women who are in menstruation, pregnant or nursing are not required to observe the fasting but are required to make up the missed days later in the year. All those who are physically unable to keep the fast, they must feed a poor or needy person (minimum of two meals that they would eat themselves) for every day missed. It inculcates sympathy for those who go hungry, and increases love, sincerity, devotion and obedience to God's commandments.

Fasting requires the Muslims to live by the moral code of Islam. Without following this moral code during Ramadan, fasting is reduced to simple starvation without bringing any reward or spiritual benefit. Fasting develops patience, piety, self-restraint, God consciousness, and willpower to bear hardships. Its objective is to develop a community of God-conscious people.

It is the month of Ramadan in which the Qur'an is revealed, the Guidance for mankind, clear proofs and the criterion of Right and Wrong

Surely, the noblest of you in the sight of Allah, is he who is the most righteous

The close of the month of Fasting is marked by a festival called Eid-al-Fitr which is celebrated through giving charity to poor people in the community and congregational prayers.

5. Pilgrimage (Hajj) to Makkah, once in a lifetime. It is an obligation only on those who are physically and financially able to undertake the journey.

Over two million people go to Makkah each year from almost all the countries of the world. In fact it is a peace conference at the world level. It is meant to provide a meeting place for Muslims from the various parts of the world to exchange the progress of Islam in their respective countries and to suggest to each other working solutions of their mutual problems.

Over three million pilgrims in prayer during Hajj in the valley of Arafat near Makkah

Pilgrims are required to wear special dress to strip away the distinctions of class and culture. It provides practical training to know that the whole of mankind is a single brotherhood, and that no one has superiority over the other based on language, color, race and ethnic background, except through piety and righteousness.

Pilgrims during prayer around the Ka'bah

Hajj is performed on the 9th day of the 12th month of Islamic Calendar called Zul-Hijjah. The rites of Hajj include circling around the Ka'bah seven times counter clockwise, walking and running between the two hills called Safa and Marwa as did Hagar, the wife of the Prophet Abraham, peace be upon him, in search of water for her baby Ishmael.

Walking between the hills of Safa and Marwa during pilgrimage – a tradition of woman (wife of the Prophet Abraham, peace be upon him)

The pilgrims stand in prayer together in the wide valley of Arafat near the 'Mount of Mercy' where Adam, peace be upon him, stood to repent for his sin of disobeying God as a result of which he was expelled from paradise. God forgave his sin and now the children of Adam stand in the same place to seek forgiveness for their sins.

The close of Hajj is marked by commemorating the tradition of the Prophet Abraham, peace be upon him, when he offered his son Ishmael, peace be upon him, in sacrifice to God and God replaced his son with a lamb and accepted that great sacrifice. God mandated the followers of Abraham, peace be upon him, to sacrifice an animal on that day (10th of Zul-Hijjah, which is called Eid-al-Adha (Festival of Feast). It is celebrated with congregational prayers, sacrificing an animal (lamb, goat, cow or camel) and the exchange of gifts in the family and Muslim communities all over the world.

What is the Ka'bah?

The *Ka'bah* is the central place of worship for Muslims, located in Makkah, Saudi Arabia. This is the first House of God built by Adam (peace be upon him), the forefather of mankind. This place of worship was demolished during the great flood of Noah, peace be upon him, and rebuilt by the Prophet Abraham and his son Ishmael, peace be upon them. This is a cube shape building in the center of sacred Mosque called Al-*Masjid Al-Haraam.*

Ka'bah in the middle of Masjid-al-Haraam

This sanctuary can accommodate over one million worshippers at a time. Every year over three million worshippers visit the Ka'bah during Hajj and Umrah (pilgrimage at anytime other than the time of Hajj).

What are Human Rights in Islam?

Islam clearly commands unqualified tolerance towards all human beings. In fact, Islam defends humanity against all criminal behavior including discrimination. The life, honor and property of all citizens in an Islamic State are considered sacred.

Islam does not seek to restrict human rights or privileges to a geographical boundary. The Prophet Muhammad, peace be upon him, reminded

everyone saying: *"O mankind you are all the children of Adam and Adam was created from dust."*

Islam has laid down some fundamental rights for humanity as a whole, which are to be respected under all circumstances whether a person is at peace with the Islamic state or at war. It opposes all those who exploit, oppress and deal unjustly with people. The Holy Qur'an very clearly states:

"O believers! Be steadfast for the sake of Allah and bear true witness and let not the enmity of a people incite you to do injustice; do justice; that is nearer to piety. Fear Allah, surely, Allah is fully aware of all your actions."   *Al-Qur'an 5:8*

Freedom of choice is laid down in the Qur'an, saying:

"There is no compulsion in religion."
Al-Qur'an 2:256

This principle is the basis for establishing universal peace. Islam integrates races and colors and encourages tolerance, friendliness and compassion among human beings. This humanitarianism is easily discerned in the general Islamic principles. God says:

"O mankind! We created you from a single (pair) of a male and a female, and made you into nations and tribes, that you may know each other (not that you may despise each other)."   *Al-Qur'an 49: 13*

Islam protects all noble values and human rights. Freedom, equality, justice, and the right to life, liberty, and security of person are of prime concern in Islamic law.

"Whosoever kills a human being for other than manslaughter or corruption in the

earth, it shall be as if he had killed all mankind, and whosoever saves the life of one, it shall be as if he had saved the life of all mankind. . ."   Al-Qur'an 5:32

Good is the reward for the righteous people in this world and the home of the hereafter will be even better, and splendid will be the home for the righteous

Islam places great emphasis on social justice and does not permit to oppress men, women, children, old people, orphans, the sick or the wounded. Women's honor and chastity are to be respected under all circumstances. The hungry person must be fed, the wounded and sick must be provided medical treatment irrespective of whether they belong to the Muslim community or from among the enemies. Human rights have been granted by God, not by any king or legislative assembly. No legislative assembly or government has the right or authority to amend, change or abrogate the rights conferred by God. These rights include:

- The Security of Life and Property
- The Protection of Honor
- Sanctity and Security of Private Life
- The Security of Personal Freedom
- The Right to Protest Against Tyranny
- Freedom of Expression
- Freedom of association
- Freedom of Conscience and Conviction

- Protection of Religious Sentiments
- Protection from Arbitrary Imprisonment
- The right to Basic Necessities of Life
- Equality before Law – Rulers are not above Law
- The right to participate in the Affairs of State

Hold fast to the rope of Allah all together and be not divided among yourselves

The verdict of the Holy Qur'an is very clear and unequivocal: *"Those who do not judge by what God has sent down, they are the disbelievers ... they are the transgressors ...they are the wrong doers."*   Al-Qur'an 5:44, 46 and 47

What does Islam say about Justice?

Islam stresses the use of justice, even if it be against one's own interest. Here is what the Holy Qur'an says about justice:

O believers! Stand firm for justice and bear true witness for the sake of Allah, even though it be against yourselves, your parents or your relatives. It does not matter whether the party is rich or poor - Allah is the well wisher of both. So let not your selfish desires swerve you from justice. If you distort your testimony or decline to give it, then you should remember that Allah is fully aware of your actions. ."   *Al-Qur'an 4:135*

O believers! Be steadfast for the sake of Allah and bear true witness and let not the enmity of a people incite you to do injustice; do justice; that is nearer to piety. Fear Allah, surely, Allah is fully aware of all your actions.   *Al-Qur'an 5:8*

"...Cooperate with one another in righteousness and piety, and do not cooperate in sin and transgression. Have fear of Allah. Allah is stern in punishment."   *Al-Qur'an 5:2*

Islam stands for peace and peace cannot be achieved without establishing justice. Therefore, Islam requires all Muslims to strive for establishing justice in the land.

Islam commands Muslims to stand up against injustice, oppression, poverty, ignorance, racism, bigotry and intolerance everywhere in the world. Without justice, rights are denied, victims are created, anger gives way to anarchy and extremism in its different forms gains more ground. We have had enough wars, crimes, terror and anger in human history. Now, it is time to identify the root causes and find solutions without partiality and favoritism.

What is Jihad in Islam?

In Islam, peace is the rule while war is the exception. Peace is a preamble to the principle of harmony in the universe, the laws of life and the origin of man, while war is the result of violations of harmony such as injustice, despotism and corruption. Islam eliminates almost all reasons that normally incite war and abolishes all wars for unjust gain and oppression.

Jihad, which is often confused with fighting and war, actually means "to struggle or to strive." *Jihad* is of three kinds. The first and primary form of Jihad is *'Jihad Alan-Nafs,'* the personal struggle against one's own shortcomings. Second is *'Jihad Alash-Shaitān,'* the struggle against the temptations of Satan. Third is *'Jihad Alal-Kufr,'* the struggle against those who do not let the Muslims live in accordance with the Commandments of God *(Allah)* and the traditions of the Prophet Muhammad, *peace be upon him.* Under this category of Jihad Islam allows the fighting in self-defense and in defense of religion or on the part of those who have been expelled forcibly from their homes. Islam condemns fighting which is based on:

- Racism, as contrary to the principles of the oneness of humanity.
- Ambition and exploitation. It does not permit war which aims at capturing markets, acquiring materials or exploiting human labor and resources. In fact, Islam looks at humanity as one big cooperative family and a part of a universal unity. It ordains all believing people to cooperate in realizing universal welfare and in abstaining from doing wrong. Islamic jurisprudence promises all humans absolute equality and justice

regardless of race, sex, or creed.
- Ostentation, the purpose of which is to magnify the pride and pomp of kings.

Islam allows fighting as the last resort when human rights are violated, propagation of God's Message to mankind is obstructed and diplomatic solutions have failed to solve these oppressions. Islam lays down strict rules of combat and prohibits harming civilians, monks, priests, nuns, old people, women and young children who are unable to fight. Islam also prohibits destroying the crops, trees, livestock and looting which usually follows conquest:

"Fight in the cause of God with those who fight against you, but do not transgress the limits. God does not like the transgressors." Al-Qur'an 2:190

"If your enemy is inclined towards peace, do make peace with them, and put your trust in God. He is the One Who hears all and knows all." Al-Qur'an 8:61

What is Hijaab (Islamic Dress Code)?

People usually discuss 'hijaab' in the context of women. However, the Qur'an, first mentions hijaab (dress code) for men before hijaab (dress code) for the women:

"Enjoin the believing men to lower their gaze and guard their modesty; that is chaster for them. Surely, Allah is well aware of their actions."

Then the hijaab for women is mentioned in the next verse:

"Likewise, enjoin the believing women to lower their gaze and guard their modesty; not to display their beauty and ornaments except what normally appears thereof; let them draw their veils over their bosoms and not display their adornment except to their husbands, their fathers, their fathers-in-law, their own sons, their stepsons, their own brothers, their nephews on either brothers' or sisters' sides, their own womenfolk, their own slaves, male attendants who lack sexual desires or small children who have no carnal knowledge of women. Also enjoin them not to strike their feet in order to draw attention to their hidden trinkets. And O believers! Turn to Allah in repentance, all of you (about your past mistakes), so that you may attain salvation." Al-Qur'an 24:30-31

Islam requires both men and women to dress simply, modestly, and with dignity. A man must always wear loose and unrevealing clothes from his navel to his knee. This is the absolute minimum covering required. He must never, for example, go out in public wearing a short which does not meet the minimum requirement. A woman must cover all her body with loose and unrevealing clothing except her face and hands. When leaving the home she

should also cover her hair obscuring the details of her body from the public. The wisdom behind this dress code is to minimize sexual enticement and degradation in society as much as possible for both men and women.

In men's clothing and adornment,

Islam seriously considers the principles of decency, modesty, chastity and manliness. Any clothing or adornment incompatible with the attainment, maintenance and development of these qualities are prohibited in Islam. Clothing materials, which stimulate arrogance or false pride, are strictly prohibited. This is the reason why Islam warns men not to use certain clothing materials, such as pure silk, and wearing certain adornment, such as gold.

The Islamic dress code applies to both women and men. It sets expectations of moral and respectful interactions between the genders. As a result both men and women are liberated from their baser instincts to focus on higher pursuits. Islamic dress takes on many beautiful forms, reflecting cultural diversity from all over the world.

Islam allows woman to use those things which are forbidden for men but are suitable for the feminine nature. When a girl reaches the age of puberty, she should cover her body except face and hands. The manner in which women should dress, beautify, walk, talk and even look is a very delicate question, and Islam pays special attention to the matter. Islam teaches that the consequences of immodesty fall not only on the individual but also upon the society that permits women and men to mingle freely, display themselves, and compete or allure one another through sexual attraction.

How does Islam view family life?

Family in Islam is the foundation of society. The family provides security and opportunity for the spiritual and material growth of its members. The family bond entails mutual expectations of rights and obligations that are prescribed by religion, enforced by law, and observed by the family members. Accordingly, the family members share certain mutual commitments. These pertain to identity and provision, inheritance and counsel, affection for the young and security for the aged, and maximization of effort to ensure the family continuity in peace. Children are considered to be the main treasure of the family.

Say: "O my Lord! Forgive, have Mercy; You are the Best of those who show mercy!"

Mutual alliance, clientele, private consent to sexual intimacy, and "common law" or "trial marriages" are not acceptable in Islam. Islam builds the family on solid grounds to provide reasonable continuity, true security, and mature intimacy. Islam recognizes that there is no more natural relationship than that of blood, and no more wholesome pattern of sexual intimacy than one in which morality and gratification are joined.

Islam recognizes the religious virtue, the social necessity, and the moral advantages of marriage. The normal course of behavior for the Muslim individual is to be family oriented and to seek a family of their own. There are many passages in the Qur'an and statements by the Prophet

Muhammad, peace be upon him, which go as far as to say that when a Muslim marries, he or she has thereby perfected half of their religion; so let them be God-conscious and careful with the other half.

Muslim scholars have interpreted the Qur'an to mean that marriage is a religious duty, a moral safeguard, and a social commitment. As a religious duty, it must be fulfilled; but like all other duties in Islam, it is enjoined only upon those who are capable of meeting the responsibilities involved.

What is the Status of Women in Islam?

Islam regards man and woman as two components of humanity, one completing the other. Woman is half of humanity and man is the other half. Both play a part in performing the functions of humanity and, in fact, one without the other is incomplete and cannot function properly for the purposes of humanity. Thus, both are complementary as well as supplementary to one another in life. Any program of life ignoring one of these components, man or woman, will be defective and incomplete. Therefore, it is not practical to form a society consisting of only women or only men. They are dependent on each other, man cannot become independent of woman, nor can woman ever live a full and complete life without man. Both need each other, not only for sexual relationship, but also for emotional satisfaction, as well as for companionship.

Seeking knowledge is the obligation of every Muslim, male or female. The type of knowledge that is most emphasized is religious knowledge. It is also required within a society to have professionals of both genders available for the benefit of the public; such as doctors, teachers, counselors, social workers.

In Islam, a woman has the right to own, inherit and dispose of her property as she likes. At the time of marriage dowry given by groom to the bride is for her personal use and she keeps her own family name rather than taking her husband's. She has the right to vote and voice her opinion even in the affairs of government.

God enjoins good conduct toward women from birth to death. Verbal, psychological, emotional, sexual, and physical violence are forbidden, as are false allegations against women's chastity and honor. God has declared in the Holy Qur'an:

"Anyone who does righteous deeds, whether a male or a female - provided he or she is a believer - shall enter paradise and no injustice will be done to them, even to the size of a speck." Al-Qur'an 4:124

What is Marriage in Islam?

In Islam marriage is a simple legal contract between a man and a woman to live together as husband and wife. In this contract either party is free to include conditions. A Muslim girl cannot be forced to marry against her will; parents simply suggest a young man that they think may be suitable for her, and she is free to choose.

Marriage is strongly encouraged and is based on mutual love and respect. It is both a legal agreement and a sacred bond. God has commanded in the Holy Qur'an:

"Get the singles among you married as well as those who are fit for marriage among your male slaves and female slaves. If they are poor, Allah will make them free from want out of His grace: for Allah has boundless resources and is All-Knowing."
Al-Qur'an 24:32

"And of His signs is that He created for you mates from among yourselves that you may find comfort with them, and He planted love and mercy for each other in your hearts; surely, there are signs in this for those who think about it."
Al-Qur'an 30:21

A woman has the same right to own property, earn wealth and spend it as a man has. Her wealth does not become the property of her husband after marriage or divorce. A woman does not have to change her last name as a result of marriage.

Husbands and wives are protectors of each other. They are equal partners and best of friends, remaining faithful to one another. The husband provides, maintains, protects and is responsible for the family. He fulfills his duties with consultation and kindness. If couples are unable to live with' one another peacefully, amicable divorce is permitted as a last resort. Divorce, even though permitted and simple, is not common in Muslim families. In case of divorce mothers are given priority in the custody of young children and the father is required to provide child support.

The Prophet Muhammad, peace be upon him, has said: *"The best among the believers is he who is best in manner and kindest to his wife."*

Why is 'More than One Wife' permitted in Islam?

Islam is for all societies and for all times to come, therefore, it accommodates various different social requirements. To have more than one wife is neither mandatory nor encouraged, but merely permitted. The reason for permission to marry more than one is compassion and support toward widows and orphans. Even in such a situation, the permission is far more restricted than the normal practice, which existed at the time of the Prophet, peace be upon him, among the Arabs and other people who married as many as ten or more wives.

Dealing justly with one's wives is an obligation. This applies to housing, food, clothing and kind treatment. If one is not sure of being able to deal justly with more than one, the Qur'an says:

"Then (marry) only one." Al-Qur'an 4:3

There was no restriction on marriages before this commandment. This commandment puts a restriction on the number of wives even in exceptional cases. The requirement of justice between the wives ruled out the fantasy that a man can have as many wives as he pleases. God-conscious men do not marry more than one if they are unable to do justice between them. That's why more than one wife is an exception among Muslims and not a general rule. Marriage in Islam is a legal contract and it is not valid unless both contracting parties consent to it. Thus no woman can be forced or "given" to a man who is already married against her will.

What does Islam say about Parents and the Elderly?

Islam puts great emphasis on the status and honor of parents and elderly folk. Parents are next only to God Almighty when it comes to respect, obedience and honor. God says in the Qur'an:

"Your Lord has decreed to you that: You shall worship none but Him, and you shall be kind to your parents; if one or both of them live to their old age in your lifetime, you shall not say to them any word of contempt nor repel them and you shall address them in kind words. You shall lower to them your wings of humility and pray: 'O Lord! Bestow on them Your blessings just as they cherished me when I was a little child.' Your Lord knows best what is in your hearts. If you do good deeds, certainly He is most forgiving to those who turn to Him in repentance."
Al-Qur'an 17:23-25

God did not give any one a choice to select children or parents. This choice is made by God Himself, therefore, He wants everyone to honor His choice by putting the requirement of obeying the parents immediately after commanding the human being to obey Him. He has commanded the believers to be kind to their parents and make a prayer of forgiveness for their parents, their children and believers at large.

In Islam, there is no room for nursing homes for elderly people. Taking care of the elderly is considered an honor and blessing. Mothers are particularly honored; the Prophet, peace be upon him, said: "Paradise lies under the feet of your mother." Serving one's parents is a duty second only to prayer, and it is their right to expect it. When parents reach old age, Muslims are required to treat them with mercy, kindness and selflessness. All elderly people of the community enjoy the similar respect and honor.

Our Lord! Forgive me and my parents and all believers on the Day when accountability will take place.

Mothers have a special place of honor and respect in Islam. A man once came to the Prophet Muhammad, peace be upon him, and asked: "O Messenger of God! Who among the people is most worthy of my good companionship?" The Prophet, peace be upon him, replied: "Your mother." The man then asked who is next, the Prophet, peace be upon him, replied "Your mother." The man repeated the question a third time and got the same answer. The man asked once again, "Who is next? Only then did the Prophet, peace be upon him, said "Your father."

What does Islam say about Food?

Science tells us that whatever one eats, it has an effect on one's behavior. This is one of the reasons that Islam prohibits the eating of carnivorous animals like lion, tiger, leopard, etc. who are violent and ferocious. The consumption of the meat of such animals would probably make a person violent and ferocious. Islam only allows the eating of herbivorous animals like cow, goat, sheep, which are peaceful and docile.

The Prophet, peace be upon him, prohibited the eating of wild animals with canine teeth and meat eating carnivorous animals such as lions, tigers, cats, dogs, wolfs, and hyenas and certain rodents like mice, rats, and rabbits with claws. Also reptiles like snakes and alligators. Birds of prey with talons or claws, like vultures, eagle, crows and owl are also prohibited.

Islam requires that in order to maintain a pure heart and a sound mind, to nourish an aspiring soul and a clean healthy body, special attention should be given to the diet on which man lives. The general principle of Islam in this respect is that all those things, which are pure and good for men and women, are lawful, as long as they are taken in moderate quantities. And all those things, which are impure, bad or harmful, are unlawful under all ordinary circumstances. There is always room and flexibility for exceptions to meet cases of absolute necessity.

Beyond this general principle, there are certain foods and drinks specified by God as forbidden. Among these are: meat of dead animals and birds, the flesh of swine and that of any animal which is slaughtered with the invocation of any name other than that of God. The Prophet said: "Your body has rights over you," and at another time he said, "No one is given any gift

better than health." Wholesome food and leading a healthy life style are considered religious obligations. The drinks which Islam considers harmful and destructive to the human spirit and morality as well as to the physique are included in the Qur'anic verse which forbids all intoxicants and all forms of gambling or games of chance.

What does Islam say about Intoxicants and Gambling?

In the prohibition of intoxicants and gambling, Islam stands unique among all religions and among all systems.

"O believers! Intoxicants and gambling (games of chance), dedication to stones (paying tribute to idols) and using arrows (for seeking luck or decision) are the filthy works of Satan. Get away from them, so that you may prosper. Satan desires to stir up enmity and hatred between you with intoxicants and gambling, to prevent you from the remembrance of Allah and from Salah (prayers). Will you not abstain? Obey Allah and obey the Messenger and abstain from these things. If you do not, then you should know that Our Messenger's duty is only to convey My message clearly."

Al-Qur'an 5:90-92

These vices have ruined innumerable lives, shattered multitudes of homes, and caused more misery to mankind than all other vices put together.

In Islam, drinking alcohol is a serious crime. A drunkard in intoxication is deprived of making the distinction between right and wrong, virtue and vice, good and evil. His actions can result into enmity and hatred, which disturb the peace and tranquillity of the society. Gambling is also a sin which destroys wealth. These moral vices are injurious to the healthy atmosphere of the society.

What Islam says about Business Interaction?

God has provided guidance about all aspects of human life including business interaction. Here is what the Holy Qur'an says about business transactions:

"O believers! When you deal with each other in lending for a fixed period of time, put it in writing. Let a scribe write it down with justice between the parties. The scribe, who is given the gift of literacy by Allah, should not refuse to write; he is under obligation to write. Let him who incurs the liability (debtor) dictate, fearing Allah his Rabb and not diminishing anything from the settlement. If the borrower is mentally unsound or weak or is unable to dictate himself, let the guardian of his interests dictate for him with justice. Let two witnesses from among you bear witness to all such documents, if two men cannot be found, then one man and two women of your choice should bear witness, so that if one of the women forgets anything the other may remind her. The witnesses must not refuse when

they are called upon to do so. You must not be averse to writing (your contract) for a future period, whether it is a small matter or big. This action is more just for you in the sight of Allah, because it establishes stronger evidence and is the best way to remove all doubts; but if it is a common commercial transaction concluded on the spot among yourselves, there is no blame on you if you do not put it in writing. You should have witnesses when you make commercial transactions. Let no harm be done to the scribe or witnesses; and if you do so, you shall be guilty of transgression. Fear Allah; it is Allah that teaches you and Allah has knowledge of everything."

Al-Qur'an 2:282

What is the concept of God in Islam?

Islam tells us that God, Who created the whole of universe, is One. His personal name is *Allah*. Nothing else can be called *Allah*. The term has no plural gender. This shows its uniqueness as compared to the term 'god,' which can be made plural, gods or feminine, goddess.

Allah is the Light of the heavens and the earth

To a Muslim *Allah* is the Almighty, Creator and Sustainer of the universe, Who is similar to nothing and nothing is comparable to Him.

He depends on none but everything else, which exists, depends on Him; neither has He begotten any child nor is He Himself the child of anyone. There is no one else that can be said to be parallel or equal to Him. He is the First, and He is the Last. He is the ultimate goal of all that exists in this universe.

Say: "He is Allah the One and Only; Allah is the Self-Sufficient (independent of all, while all are dependent on Him); He begets not, nor is He begotten (he has no child, nor is He a child of any one); and there is none comparable to Him."
Al-Qur'an 112:1-4

Islam rejects characterizing God in any human form or depicting Him as favoring certain individuals or nations on the basis of wealth, power or race. He created all human beings as equals. They may distinguish themselves and obtain His favor only through virtue and piety.

The concept that God rested on the seventh day of creation, that God wrestled with one of His soldiers, that God is an envious plotter against mankind, or that God is incarnate in any human being are considered blasphemy from the Islamic point of view.

The unique belief in the One God (Allah) is a reflection of Islam's emphasis on the purity of the belief in God, which is the essence of the message of all His Prophets. Because of this, Islam considers associating any deity or personality with God as a deadly sin, which God will never forgive, despite the fact that He may forgive all other sins.

Surely, Allah does not forgive shirk (associating any partner with Him); and may forgive sins other than that if He so pleases. This is because one, who commits shirk with Allah, does indeed invent a great sinful lie.   Al-Qur'an 4:48

Surely Allah will never forgive the one who commits shirk (worships anyone other than Him); and may forgive anyone else, if He so pleases. One who commits shirk has indeed gone far away from the Right Way.   Al-Qur'an 4:116

He (Allah) has power over every thing

God has the power to do whatever He wills. He is Ever-Living. He is the Giver of life. The Love of God for His creatures is immense and beyond human imagination. Mankind cannot measure or count the favors of God. He creates men and women in the best form of creation and gives them all the senses and faculties that they need for their growth. He creates the mind to understand, the soul and conscience to be good and righteous, and the feelings and sentiments to be kind and humane. The mercy of God gives men and women hope and peace, courage and confidence. It enables them to remedy their grief and sorrows, to overcome their difficulties and obtain success and happiness. Indeed, the mercy of God relieves the distressed, cheers the afflicted, consoles the sick, strengthens the desperate, and comforts the needy.

What is the concept of Life in Islam?

Life is a brilliant demonstration of God's wisdom and knowledge, and a vivid reflection of His art and power. He is the Giver and Creator of life. Nothing comes into existence by chance. Life is a dear and cherishable asset, and no sensible or normal person would like to lose it by choice. Life is given to mankind by God, and He is the only Rightful Owner to take it back. This is why Islam forbids all kinds of suicide and self-destruction, and recommends patience and good faith when a dear soul passes away. When a murderer is executed in punishment, his life is taken away by the right of God and in accordance with His Law. It is a tragedy that the secular and the religious, the scientific and the spiritual seem to be in conflict in secular societies. Islam puts an end to this conflict and brings harmony in all these aspects of human life.

When God gives life to men and women, it is not in vain that He endows them with unique qualities and great abilities. Nor is it in vain that He charges them with certain obligations.

God means to help man to fulfill the purpose of life and realize the goal of existence. He means to help him to learn the creative art of living and enjoy the good taste of life according to Divine guidance. Life is a trust from God, and men and women are trustees who should handle this trust with consciousness of responsibility to Him.

We have indeed created man in the best stature

Life may be likened to a journey starting from a certain point and ending at a certain destination. It is a transitory stage, an introduction to the Eternal Life in the Hereafter. In this journey, men and women are travelers and should be concerned with only what is of use to them in the Future Life. In other words, they should do all the good they can and make themselves fully prepared to move any minute to Eternal Life. They should consider their life on earth as a chance provided for them to make the best of it while they can, because when their time to leave comes they can never delay it for one moment. If their term expires, it will be too late to do anything about it or extend it. The best use of life, therefore, is to live it according to the teachings of God and make it a safe passage to the future Eternal Life. Islam has laid down a complete system of regulations and principles to show man how to live it, what to take and what to leave, what to do and what to shun, and so on. In one of his comprehensive statements Prophet Muhammad, peace be upon him, wisely advised man to consider himself a stranger in this life or a traveler passing through this world.

What is the concept of Life after Death in Islam?

Man's life is not limited to the short span of earthly existence. This world will come to an end some day, and the dead will rise on the Day of Judgment to stand for their final and fair trial. Everyone will appear before the Almighty God and face the consequences of their deeds done in this life. Thus, life in the Hereafter is a continuation of the earthly life but different in nature.

Our Lord! Give us the good life, both in this world and in the Hereafter and save us from the torment of the fire.

Everything we do in this world, every intention we have, every move we make, every thought we entertain, and every word we say, are all counted and kept in accurate records. On the Day of Judgment, they will be brought forth. People with good records will be generously rewarded and warmly welcomed to the Paradise of God, and those with bad records will be punished and cast into Hell. The real nature of Paradise or Hell, and the exact description of them are known to God only. There are descriptions of Paradise and Hell in the Qur'an. In Paradise, said the Prophet Muhammad, peace be upon him, there are things, which no eye has ever seen, no ear has ever heard, and no mind has ever conceived.

Belief in Life after Death and man's accountability to God gives a sense and meaning to one's life and differentiates human beings from animals.

In fact, if there is no life after death, the very belief in God becomes irrelevant because God would be unjust and indifferent; having created human beings not concerned with cruelty, corruption, aggression and injustice that is going on in this world. God is just. He will punish those who are responsible for killing innocent people, creating corruption in the societies, enslaving thousands' to serve their whims. Punishment and reward equal to the evil or noble deeds of people are not possible in this short span of worldly life. Life after death will be eternal and it will be possible to reward or punish the persons to the full extent that they deserve, therefore, belief in the 'Life after Death' serves as a reminder against crime, corruption, immorality, and injustice on this earth.

What is the concept of Sin in Islam?

One of the major troublesome areas of human existence is the problem of sin or evil in the world. The belief that the first sin started with Adam and Eve during their life in the Garden of Eden.

That event led to their fall and has ever since branded the human race with guilt, stigma, and bewilderment.

Islam takes a unique position on the whole issue. The Qur'an states that Adam and Eve were directed by God to reside in the Garden of Eden and enjoy its produce as they pleased, assured of bountiful supplies and comfort.

They were warned not to approach a particular tree and not to follow the footsteps of Satan so that they would not run into harm and injustice. Satan intrigued them to temptation and caused them to forget God's prohibition, and therefore, to lose their joyful state. They were expelled from the Garden and brought down to earth to live, die, and be taken out again for the Final Judgment. Having realized what they had done, they felt shame, guilt, and remorse. They prayed for God's forgiveness and were forgiven.

The idea of Original Sin or hereditary criminality has no place in the teachings of Islam. Man, according to the Qur'an and to the Prophet, is born in a natural state of purity called fitrah (nature), which is Islam or submission to the will and law of God. After that, whatever becomes of man is the result of external influences and intruding factors. A person is innocent until he grows to an age when he can distinguish Right from Wrong. The home environment is crucial and it plays a decisive role in the formation of human personality and the development of moral character. This does not deny the individual his or her freedom of choice nor exempt him or her from responsibility, rather it is a relief from heavy burden of hereditary criminality or instinctual sin.

According to the moral scale of Islam, it is not a sin to be imperfect or fallible. This is part of human nature as a finite limited creature. But it is a sin if a person has the ways and means of relative perfection and chooses not to seek it. A sin is any act, thought, or will that is:

1. Deliberate
2. Defies the unequivocal law of God
3. Violates the rights of God or the rights of man
4. Harmful to the soul or body
5. Normally avoidable
6. Committed repeatedly

These are the components of sin, which are not innate or hereditary. It is true that men and women have the potential of sin latent in them, but this is not beyond their capacity of piety and goodness. If they choose to actualize the potential of sin, instead of the potential of goodness, they will be adding a new external element to their pure nature. For this added external element man alone is responsible.

O Allah! I ask You to provide me a good life and let me die on the Right Path

Allah has told the Greatest Truth

SOME USEFUL BOOKS FOR
Reading about Islam, Qur'an and Seerah

Al-QUR'AN, The Guidance for Mankind, by Muhammad Farooq-i-Azam Malik , The Institute of Islamic Knowledge, P. O. Box 8307, Houston, Texas 77288-8307

MUHAMMAD: His Life Based on the Earliest Sources, by Martin Lings Inner Traditions International, One Park Street, Rochester, Vermont 05767

The AUTOBIOGRAPHY OF MALCOLM X as told to Alex Haley, Random House, Inc., 1745 Broadway NY, New York. 10126

DAUGHTERS OF ANOTHER PATH (Experiences of American Women Choosing Islam), by Carol Anway, Yawna Publications, P.O. Box 27, Lee's Summit, Missouri 64063

THE FAMILY STRUCTURE IN ISLAM, by Hammudah Abd al Ati, American Trust Publications, 745 McClintock Drive, #314, Burr Ridge, Illinois 60527

JIHAD: A Commitment to Universal Peace, by Marcel A. Boisard, American Trust Publications, 745 McClintock Drive, #314, Burr Ridge, Illinois 60527

THE VISION OF ISLAM, by Sachiko Murata and William Chittick, Paragon House, 370 Lexington Avenue, NY, New York 10017

WHAT ISLAM IS ALL ABOUT (Student Textbook), by Yahiya Emerick, IBTS, P.O. Box 5153, Long Island City, New York 11105

READING THE MUSLIM MIND, by Dr. Hassan Hathout, Islamic Center of Southern California, 434 South Vermont, CA 90020

We hope you like this Booklet, to improve, add more topics, sponsor
its printing cost or to get copies for free distribution, please
contact the Institute at the following address:

THE INSTITUTE OF ISLAMIC KNOWLEDGE
P. O. Box 8703, Houston, Texas 77288-8307
Tel: 281-448-4080 • Fax: 713-526-9090
www.al-quraan.org

ISBN 0-98194390-

9 780981 943909

This Booklet is distributed by:

Flint Islamic Center
9447 Corunna Road, Swartz Creek, MI 48473
Tel: 810-922-6854
And
Grand Blanc Islamic Center
1479 E. Baldwin Road, Grand Blanc, MI 48439
Tel: 810-603-9920

For more information:
Please call: 1-800-662-4752 (10am – 10pm)
Or
Log on to: www.gainpeace.com

Activities at the Flint Islamic Center:

Radio program on "AM 1570" - every Sunday
4:00 PM to 6:00 PM
Friday Service 1:45 PM to 2:45 PM - Open to Public
Islamic Study Circle every Friday 6:30 PM to 8:00 PM
Open House - come and taste Middle Eastern food
On February 07, 2009 at 5:30 PM

The Institute of Islamic Knowledge
P.O. Box 8307 • Houston, TX. 77288
Tel: 281.448.4080 • Fax: 713.526.9090